ANIMAL FACT

Credits— Photos: Front cover: Marco Kopp; Back cover: Todd Smith; inside front: Mark Stevens; inside back: Gerald Blair.
Sequence: Image Bank/Getty Images.

ANIMAL FACT

Bald eagles can be found in every
American state except Hawaii.

ANIMAL FACT

Bald eagles are social animals,
and tend to gather in large groups,
especially in the winter.

ANIMAL FACT

Bald eagles tend to live and nest near
the coast in pine forests, or near
rivers, lakes and wet prairies.

ZOOFLIPZ™

ANIMAL FACT

Bald eagles live near water
so they can be close to
their favorite food: fish!

ZOOFLIPZ™

ANIMAL FACT

Bald eagles are considered to be
scavengers as much as hunters.

ZOOFLIPZ™

ANIMAL FACT

Bald eagles spot their prey
using their keen eyesight.

ZOOFLIPZ™

ANIMAL FACT

Gliding over the water's surface,
a bald eagle snatches
its prey in its sharp talons.

ZOOFLIPZ™

ANIMAL FACT

If no fish are available, a bald
eagle might eat a duck, muskrat,
turtle, rabbit, or even a snake.

ANIMAL FACT

Long ago, Native Americans
would look for flocks of eagles to
find out where to catch salmon.

ANIMAL FACT

Bald eagles living in the Arctic leave the cold climate in the fall to migrate south, where food is easier to find in the winter.

ANIMAL FACT

The bald eagle's name comes from
"balde," an old English term meaning
"white," for the feathers on its head.

ZOOFLIPZ™

ANIMAL FACT

The bald eagle isn't really bald.

ZOOFLIPZ™

ANIMAL FACT

Some bald eagles have a
wing span of 8 feet or more.

ANIMAL FACT

The average adult bald eagle wingspan
is between six and seven feet.

ZOOFLIPZ™

ANIMAL FACT

A bald eagle can be up to
3 feet tall when fully grown.

ANIMAL FACT

Bald eagles can live up to
30 years in the wild, and
even longer in captivity.

ANIMAL FACT

Female bald eagles are bigger
than males of the same age.

ANIMAL FACT

Adult female bald eagles
can weigh up to 15 pounds.

ANIMAL FACT

Bald eagles usually mate for life.

ANIMAL FACT

Adult bald eagles often nest within 100
miles of where they hatched.

ANIMAL FACT

A bald eagle's nest can be
up to 9 feet in diameter.

ZOOFLIPZ™

ANIMAL FACT

Once, a bald eagle nest was
found that was 34 years old
and weighed over two tons!

ZOOFLIPZ™

ANIMAL FACT

A bald eagle's nest can
weigh hundreds of pounds!

ZOOFLIPZ™

ANIMAL FACT

Bald eagles usually lay eggs from
November to mid-March in warm areas,
and late winter through spring in cold.

ANIMAL FACT

Though they can lay one to three eggs,
bald eagles usually lay two.

ZOOFLIPZ™

ANIMAL FACT

Bald eagles' eggs
incubate for 31 to 45 days.

ZOOFLIPZ™

ANIMAL FACT

Both bald eagle parents help
take care of their eggs and
rear their young.

ZOOFLIPZ™

ANIMAL FACT

Eaglets' feathers turn dark
brown before they leave the
nest, at about 12 weeks of age.

ANIMAL FACT

Eaglets have light gray feathers
when they are born.

ANIMAL FACT

Newly hatched eagles
are called "eaglets."

ZOOFLIPZ™

ANIMAL FACT

Juvenile bald eagles have white patches on
their underside and tail, but don't get their
white heads until they are 4-6 years old.

ANIMAL FACT

Bald eagles have
yellow beaks and legs.

ANIMAL FACT

The bald eagle was selected by our
founders to be the national bird because it
is a species unique to North America.

ANIMAL FACT

The bald eagle was declared the National
Emblem of the United States by the
Continental Congress in 1782.

ANIMAL FACT

Benjamin Franklin wanted the
wild turkey, not the bald eagle,
to be America's national bird!

ZOOFLIPZ™

ANIMAL FACT

To swim, bald eagles use their
wings in an overhand motion that
looks like the butterfly stroke.

ZOOFLIPZ™

ANIMAL FACT

Bald eagles can swim!

ANIMAL FACT

The bald eagle is called a *riparian* species. This means it lives near water.

ZOOFLIPZ™

ANIMAL FACT

Eagles can catch flying birds by
turning upside-down in mid-air, but
this doesn't happen very often.

ANIMAL FACT

Bald eagles communicate
through a variety of vocalizations.

ZOOFLIPZ™

ANIMAL FACT

A bald eagle can dive at speeds
of over 100 miles per hour!

ANIMAL FACT

A bald eagle can fly 20 to 40
miles per hour in normal flight.

ANIMAL FACT

Most of the nesting bald eagles
in the continental United States
are found in Florida.

ZOOFLIPZ™

ANIMAL FACT

There are almost 6,000
breeding pairs of bald eagles
in the continental United States.

ZOOFLIPZ™

ANIMAL FACT

The eagle has played an important
role in American art, folklore,
music, and even architecture.

ANIMAL FACT

Federal protection and breeding programs
have been instrumental in the bald eagle's
recovery from critical population decline.

ANIMAL FACT

There are approximately 100,000
bald eagles alive today in the wild.